SAVE OUR BIRDS

The item should be returned or renewed by the last date stamped below.

Newport
CITY COUNCIL
CYNGOR DINAS
Casnewydd

Dylid dychwelyd neu adnewyddu'r eitem erbyn y dyddiad olaf sydd wedi'i stampio isod.

To renew visit / Adnewyddwch ar
www.newport.gov.uk/libraries

SAVE OUR BIRDS

HOW TO BRING OUR FAVOURITE BIRDS BACK FROM THE BRINK OF EXTINCTION

MATT SEWELL

EBURY
PRESS

Published in 2021 by Ebury Press an imprint of Ebury Publishing,
20 Vauxhall Bridge Road,
London SW1V 2SA

Ebury Press is part of the Penguin Random House group
of companies whose addresses can be found at
global.penguinrandomhouse.com

Penguin
Random House
UK

Production: Sian Pratley
Editor: Camilla Ackley

This edition first published by Ebury Press in 2021

www.penguin.co.uk

A CIP catalogue record for this book is available
from the British Library

ISBN 9781529107944

Printed and bound in China by Toppan Leefung Ltd

The authorised representative in the EEA is Penguin Random House
Ireland, Morrison Chambers, 32 Nassau Street, Dublin D02 YH68

Penguin Random House is committed to a sustainable future for our
business, our readers and our planet. This book is made from
Forest Stewardship Council® certified paper.

For Romy & Mae

CONTENTS

FOREWORD

BY

MELISSA HARRISON

Imagine a garden entirely without birds. Imagine
a whole street empty of them — worse, a town with
no spring nests or morning birdsong, no swifts or
swallows overhead on hot days, its back-garden bird
feeders entirely unvisited, and each tree's welcoming
cradle of branches vacant, untenanted, and still.

Actually, don't: it's far too horrible. Nobody wants
to live without birds, our lovely, feathered familiars
since the dawn of humankind. Yet that's where we
could be heading if we don't change course —
and soon.

It's a bit too much to think about, isn't it? Especially
now. But the good news is this: not only can we
turn things around — by which I mean *you*, and
you (and me!) — but doing so is going to be
loads of fun.

It all starts with curiosity: what's out there, and what's it up to? What's it doing now, and why? In my experience, connecting with the natural world makes our world bigger and more beautiful — more rewarding to be in, too.

I've found that imaginatively enlarging our world to include our fellow creatures leads pleasurably and naturally to care and custodianship. 'This new thing I care about,' we find ourselves thinking, 'what does it need? And how can I help?'

Action born of love is joyful and easy; it rewards us tenfold and is never a drain. I hope this book will help you to really see the birds around you — and more importantly, the ones that aren't — so that your own journey to custodianship can begin.

Melissa Harrison

INTRODUCTION

For those of us that love the natural world, the times we are currently living through can seem scary and bewildering. With news headlines spreading fear while mass protests and environmental movements appear to be doing little to incite real change, it can be hard not to feel overwhelmed and helpless. The concept of climate change can be difficult to fathom — in Britain we can travel for miles and see green fields and woodland, birds in the trees and in the sky. But does this really provide us with the whole picture of what is happening on our watch?

Some of the UK's most iconic birds have recently been placed on The IUCN's Red List. This list was established in 1964 and has become the world's most comprehensive source of information on the global extinction risk status of animals, plant species and fungi. The list currently includes species such as the Nightingale, Skylark, Curlew and House Sparrow. These amazing birds sit in uncomfortable proximity to other once plentiful, now threatened species, such as the Puffin, Lapwing, Turtle Dove, Yellowhammer and many, many more.

There are many complex reasons for the drastic
fall in numbers of these listed UK species, but
certainly one major contributing factor is habitat
loss. However, comprehending the concept of habitat
loss is not as straightforward. We can see that there
are fields, trees and rivers — what is less obvious
is the loss of abundance of biodiversity, the loss of
breeding grounds, and the absence of specific food
which, alongside other hidden effects of climate
change, are dramatically harming nature in our own
countryside and even in our own backyards.

The good news is that there are many things we can
do to help, and this book will hopefully be not only
a celebration of the feathered friends that so
desperately need our attention, but also a guide to
how we can all help save our birds.

Chapter One

WOODLAND

For forest birds, an ancient woodland must feel like a city bursting with opportunities for the finest food; the best accommodation to meet all your individual requirements; and teeming with other feathered folk to sing to, including some to try your best to steer clear of. These woods are alive with the sound of birdsong, with the sweet harmonies of finch couples, the thick banter of a rookery, the spooky nocturnal calls of owls and the ever-present alarms of thrushes and tits. Birds feel as much a part of a forest as dead leaves, acorns, fungi and rope swings. But sadly, some woods are now deathly quiet that you can hear a pine needle drop. This is often due to the planting of fast-growing and often non-native conifer and pine trees. They might be perfect for timber production and cash turnover, but not quite so perfect for our birds that need the insects, nesting places and ecosystems that thrive in mixed and broad-leafed forests. Yes, we need more trees planted (in the right places!) but more importantly, we need to protect the ancient woodland that we already have, the citadels for our native birds.

Nightingale

Luscinia megarhynchos

To catch the song of the Nightingale is a deep pleasure.
Heard during the day the melody can easily be lost in
the gossip of other small passerines and the woodland
ambience surrounding it. But the song takes on a whole
new feel when heard during the cover of darkness in
woodland, when few other songbirds are up, as the
melodic phrases are punctuated by the silence between
verses, the song feels like an effervescent 'I am me,
I am here, and I am free.' Which, for quite an un-
enigmatic-looking bird, is a mighty chant. No wonder
the Nightingale has been famed throughout Europe
for centuries. Every summer our artiste travels all the
way from West Africa to breed in the south of the UK,
southern and central Europe but each year the numbers
arriving get lower and lower. Our once insect-rich
summers are a thing of the past due to pesticides and
intensive farming practices, so why should our visitor
extend its travel plans when there is simply nothing to
eat here? Sadly, the Nightingale is now singing the blues
as climate change is affecting their African wintering
grounds too and throwing everything out of whack.

Marsh & Willow Tit

Poecile palustris & Poecile montanus

Practically impossible to tell apart, the only real difference between these two is their calls and songs. For me they are almost the perfect-looking birds — it's the black cap and bib contrasted with the silvery buff of the body that really does it for me. I think they are a design classic — just like Adidas's three stripes, the anglepoise lamp or the Helvetica font. Yes, I know they are very understated, but they are perfectly formed.

Sadly, both species are in decline. They are both sedentary, meaning that they don't migrate but stay put all year round after finding their own territory in old woodland. The decline is probably driven by woodland management — the old, wet stumps needed by the Willow Tit (which digs its own nest holes), and the dead trees (with pre-drilled holes) preferred by the Marsh Tit, simply aren't on offer. As neither species is willing to travel too far in search of new and suitable habitat, the loss of corridors connecting what remains may sadly be limiting the number breeding.

Woodcock

Scolopax rusticola

These perfectly camouflaged woodland waders look like they would wheeze like a tiny set of bagpipes if you picked them up. But don't be fooled by their beaky and portly appearance, these birds are pretty sharp; cloaked in an impossible display of invisibility, there is no way you would spot a Woodcock as it rests or nests among the dead leaves on the forest floor, unless you are about to step on it, when it dramatically springs to life, up and away. Their formulaic flights of courtship above woodland at dusk — known as roding — are fast and furious. Folklore has it that a disturbed female Woodcock can courageously fly away from danger with her chicks on her back, safe from harm.

A lot of our wintering birds are from Europe and eastern Russia and they migrate here for food, shelter and a milder climate for a few months. There are millions of Woodcocks distributed around the world but, unfortunately, they are a prized shooting bird and it is the fall in numbers of breeding birds here in the UK that rings alarm bells. It is thought that this is due to habitat loss caused by over-grazing deer and the general drying out of woodland and removal of deadwood. But the monstrous fact that you can legally hunt these amazing birds is also a factor that cannot be ignored.

Lesser Spotted Woodpecker

Dryobates minor

Lesser spotted indeed! These beautiful but elusive sparrow-sized birds get most of their attention from the pages of bird books. Deliberations often occur when there is a woodpecker on the garden feeder. 'Quick, get the book!' 'Hmmm, was it a Great or Lesser Spotted?' The answer is almost always that it was the big and bold Great Spotted Woodpecker. So, the Lesser once again fades into the background and although it's featured in all the books, this charmer is so rare it could simply disappear with the turn of a page. It is rightly a difficult bird to spot, preferring to spend its days foraging high in the hidden treetops totally out of our eyeline and, like the Woodcock (see page 20), the drying and removal of dead wood by local authorities has to be considered as a cause for their decline. If we can put this knowledge of how to protect their habitat into practice, we have the power to make the Lesser Spotted a much more frequently spotted woodpecker.

Pied Flycatcher & Spotted Flycatcher
Ficedula hypoleuca & Muscicapa striata

Flycatchers are found around the world and come in all different shapes, sizes and colour formations — the Indian Paradise-flycatcher and Pale-eyed Pygmy-tyrant are personal favourites. As far as names go, the latter is hard to beat! In fact, there are over 400 species of tyrant flycatchers alone. Here in the UK, we have the migratory Pied and the (not so spotted) Spotted varieties. They may both be small and cute, but they are utter tyrants to our summer insects when they arrive from wintering in Africa. The Pied is like a pocket-sized orca in both its markings and its ferocious hunting abilities. It is not quite tossing penguins around for fun but it is incredibly adept at catching flies. Likewise, the Spotted that perches, strikes and returns to its vantage point like a ninja's yo-yo is precise and deadly.

With both birds in decline, it is hard to pinpoint what is behind them not returning to the UK and Europe. Climate change will almost certainly be affecting their migratory roots from sub-Saharan Africa, as their journey is timed to hit peak greenness and maximum insects along the way to fuel their epic flight. With the seasons being off-kilter, the flycatchers may find themselves starved of food during their voyage and arrive in the UK to a depleted food source. The last 50 years of herbicide use has also wiped out much of our flycatchers' food; there simply aren't enough flies to catch and sadly what they can catch can poison them.

Hawfinch

Coccothraustes coccothraustes

This chrome-beaked bird may look like a cyborg sent back from the future, but it is in fact a shy, heavy-billed finch. Coloured like the autumnal equinox, it dwells high in tree canopies and keeps safely out of sight. Although the Hawfinch's numbers are bolstered during our colder months by European birds seeking warmer climes, the native Hawfinch is endangered and becoming increasingly rare. Preferring to inhabit only a handful of deciduous forests across the British Isles, these birds are increasingly threatened by the deforestation of ancient woodland. They cannot adapt to change and if their woodland home is not protected but destroyed, they will only be occasional visitors and even harder to spot, and that would be an utter travesty.

Golden Oriole

Oriolus oriolus

Surely such a thing of beauty cannot herald from our stoic and workman-like isles? These golden creatures must be from the heavens! It's easy to think the beautiful Oriole must be from anywhere other than here — the Mediterranean? The Far East? Heaven? Maybe all three are true; they are definitely found all over southern Europe in the summer and they can be an exciting summertime spot in the UK as migrants spread their wings and can be spied in the least likely of places. But not too long ago some of these Golden Orioles were actually from here, born in the fens of East Anglia and reared in poplar plantations perfect for raising golden baby birds. Although the Golden Oriole has been a conservation priority for decades, sadly, they no longer breed here at all. A positive move towards protecting their fenland habitat at home, and their breeding grounds abroad, means we may well one day see these golden sunshine birds back raising young here. What a beautiful prospect that is! Certainly, something worth fighting for.

Fieldfare & Redwing

Turdus pilaris & Turdus iliacus

These thrushes are our winter friends; they arrive from the north after most of our other feathered visitors have headed south. Our Scandinavian migrants bring with them a robust and jovial attitude, arriving in great flocks, marauding rowan trees and hawthorns as they go like Vikings hungry for a feast. Luckily there is plenty of winter fare to go round before they return on the second leg of their journey in early spring. Happily, for us, some never depart and have called the UK home, with small colonies breeding up north in very, very select and small numbers. These colonies are forever at risk from an army of dangers: habitat loss and disease being the most pressing, but now climate change poses a game-changing threat to these birds. As the world gets warmer, the birds that populate certain areas are constantly moving and changing — soon even the colder north of the UK won't be suitable for these vivacious birds and they will no doubt set sail like their ancestors for more favourable lands.

Wood Warbler

Phylloscopus sibilatrix

This spritely lime-and-soda songster could easily be confused with its self-aggrandising cousin the Chiffchaff, or quite frankly any other warbler that heads to the UK from Africa as the weather starts to get warmer. The best way to spot the difference is to close your eyes, as the Chiffchaff quite gloriously sings (or rather shouts) its name from the top of a tree while the Wood Warbler's song sounds very much like a coin spinning to a stop on a table or a marble being dropped. This subtle song that forms part of the fabric of a bustling woodland is sadly becoming quieter throughout the whole of western Europe as the Warbler's numbers across the continent are declining. Like most of the birds in this book, the reasons behind this dramatic decrease are not totally understood. It may be that this ground-nesting bird's tiny eggs and young are an easy target for rodents, corvids and adventurous pets that happen across the Warbler's camouflaged grass and bluebell-knitted dome nest. Its preferred habitat of hilly deciduous forest is hard to manage and as these birds are now breeding more successfully in the north of England and Scotland it's hard not to assume that global warming is changing their preferred habitat and pushing them gradually further north.

Lesser Redpoll

Acanthis cabaret

The Lesser Redpoll may be easily one of the most unrecognisable birds on our list of threatened birds. It is one of those LBJs (Little Brown Jobs) that only real birders seem to get excited about, but I am not a twitcher (a fond birdwatching term for someone who travels far and wide to spot rare species), just a nature lover, so any bird that is even a bit pink is pretty special to me. In breeding mode, the male shows off some spectacular colours; mixes of tawny and caramel browns, antique pink and raspberry jam that is quite similar to the other pinkish finches, such as the Linnet (see page 90) and Twite (see page 140). When out of season the males return to streaky patterns similar to those of the female, making it quite difficult to distinguish them from other streaky finches, especially when they are in big social flocks, chattering away with their rattling call.

Once only found in the UK, Ireland and the Alps, the little Lesser Redpoll has spread its wings and can now be found across central mainland Europe. It is not quite known why the UK's numbers are down, but one suggestion is that their preferred breeding grounds of conifer plantations have been in decline. So, unfortunately if we don't act quickly, these birds may be packing their passports and moving abroad for good.

Nightjar

Caprimulgus europaeus

The Nightjar is a summer migrant that travels up from West Africa to breed in select locations across the country. This incredible bird seems to hail from a forgotten time; it looks part Swift, part Kestrel, part bat. The Nightjar also looks a little like the forest floor as it is a ground nester, so complex camo is needed as a disguise in the heathland where it roosts alongside coniferous woodland.

Such habitats aren't always well guarded — heathland is often threatened by development or afforestation (we don't just need to plant more trees but plant them in the right places), so the Nightjar's numbers have begun to decline in recent years. It's not all doom and gloom though!

Protection of heathland and a new respect for the importance of clear fells means that the Nightjar has tentatively left the Red List of endangered birds, moving into a lower-risk section of the list, due to these inspiring conservation efforts.

WHAT CAN WE DO?

It's easy to think that all we need to do to save our woodland birds is to plant more trees but, as you will probably find reading this book, there are no simple answers. What we really need to do is to protect the birds' preferred habitats and bolster new ones. New trees are vital, but only in the right places as trees do not create suitable habitats for all birds. Thankfully there has been a recent shift in awareness, resulting in some effective rewilding schemes (such as Rewilding Britain), pushing up like acorns around the UK. If you'd like to support schemes like these, that is an effective way of helping woodland birds in peril. Vast areas of the land in the UK are being left to be reclaimed by nature, letting trees grow to take back the landscape they once held so tightly. In time, some of these trees die and rot back, creating bustling insect communities, nesting opportunities, and, finally, woodland clearings that allow the whole process to start over again. Hopefully these interconnecting wild areas will create a haven for wildlife to thrive, as well as playing a role in climate change by soaking up huge amounts of carbon year after year. What's not to like? We just need a robust government that can see the real importance of these schemes and is dedicated to protecting nature now and for future generations. If you're interested in supporting rewilding schemes, you can visit Knepp Castle Estate, The Rewild Project, Corrour Estate and Coomeshead. Members of the public can also take a course on rewilding; both the Centre for Alternative Technology and Trees for Life run these courses.

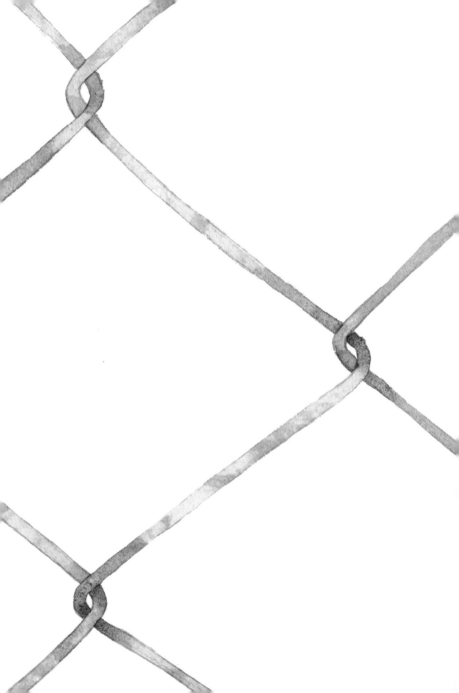

Chapter Two

URBAN

You never know what's hiding around the corner: our towns and cities can be a treasure trove of spotting opportunities if you put your phone away and look up. Mischievous Jays have followed Blackbirds and thrushes out of the woods and moved into town, and now herons and even kingfishers frequent the graffiti-lined canals of our cities. Bird feeders are a meeting place for all manner of winged friends passing between duck-filled, tree-lined parks, including a variety of finches, robins and tits as well as stars such as the Nuthatch, woodpecker and the fearsome Sparrowhawk. Nature isn't normally the reason why people move to cities but these regular sightings of the urban feathered ensemble can help us feel more connected to the natural world and put a real spring in our step.

House Sparrow
Passer domesticus

When I was very young, a male House Sparrow, affectionally named Sergeant Spuggy, would fly up from a bush and sit on my bedroom windowsill. From this vantage point he would keep a lookout and bark orders while I would gaze out from behind the reflective glass. I often drew Spuggy and he kick-started my love of birds and art. These fantastic birds are like us in so many ways; living socially, always busy and quarrelling. They seem to get everywhere, from gardens, parks and woods to farmland, car parks and even the seaside too. So why are they in decline? Building practices have changed in recent years, taking away nesting opportunities (which also affects Swallows and Swifts) and agricultural changes have meant fewer insects, which has a knock-on effect on the number of insects found in towns. There's also the possibility that herbicides and human pollutants may be affecting our sparrows. They are a good example that shows being locally abundant doesn't protect you from decline.

Black Redstart

Phoenicurus ochruros

Put simply, a lot of our birds are endangered because the UK and Europe just isn't wild enough anymore. All of our outdoor spaces are owned, managed and pumped full of chemicals to yield as much from the earth as possible. Luckily for the Black Redstart, it's a different kind of wildness that it needs to thrive, loving disused urban areas where crumbled stonework is spiked with weeds and wild flowers and alive with bugs and flies. These incredibly rare black-and-orange birds can be spotted in our busiest cities if you're lucky, and hopefully that will increasingly be the case as organisations set up green roofs to help them thrive. Wasteland and rubble in our gentrified urban areas may be a thing of the past, but let's pray our future is graced with the urban wildness of the Black Redstart.

Starling

Sturnus vulgaris

A bit of a Marmite bird. I hate the stuff, but I do love Starlings; in full breeding regalia they have a metallic sheen that glistens purple and green, embedded with dots that look like a star chart of the cosmos. They have unworldly coded songs of buzzes, bleeps and alien melodies as well as being amazing mimics; I've heard one do a very good Blackbird impression before. Individually in flight their triangular shapes aren't that head-turning, but during the colder months starlings gather in great flocks to create lava-lamp-like organic masses of pulsating black points; these murmurations are usually contrasted against dusk and are a wonder of the natural world. Unfortunately, to some starlings are just those odd, noisy brown birds, but this might be a view from the past given that there are so few around now that it would be difficult for them to cause any distress. One way in which we can help these unnatural natural wonders is by ensuring they have enough food and places to nest (see more on page 54). Small but mighty steps you can take include popping a bird feeder in your garden, or on your windowsill; Starlings love suet products, and even peanuts when placed in mesh feeders.

Song Thrush

Turdus philomelos

A classic thrush: fine voice, stark and distinct spotted markings, and the busy manner of somebody who has got a long to-do list to get through today. This songbird, like many birds, has taken a big hit outside of cities due to pesticides and the apocalyptic manicuring of the land. They are a fraction of the common sight they once were. But much like the Blackbird and the Jay, they have increasingly found refuge and made a home in town gardens and city parks. Here's hoping life will find a way and this thrush's amazing song will be heard forever more, both in urban environments and out further into the countryside.

Mistle Thrush

Turdus viscivorus

The Mistle Thrush is a very tall and business-like thrush with a mystical side. The Druids believed that mistletoe was magic and used to cut it with a golden sickle to use in ceremonies and rituals. The Mistle Thrush thinks it's pretty magic too, getting its name from the mistletoe berries it enjoys devouring so much. That said, a more practical balanced diet is needed by all birds so the loss of natural sources of food is surely contributing to the decline in these majestic thrushes. What was once a common sight in town gardens and school playing fields is now a miraculously lucky spot. A central problem in cities is non-native trees, while they may be quick growing, nice to look at and carbon friendly, they just don't support the life that is needed to feed our birds. A London plane tree can support only a handful of species, whereas an oak tree maintains hundreds. It's hard to say exactly what is driving the decline in Mistle Thrush numbers, but it is probably the same thing that is holding back the Song Thrush (see page 48) and Starling (see page 46). In fact, any bird that specialises in eating insects during the summer breeding period has a hard time on our over-manicured lawns.

Peregrine Falcon

Falco peregrinus

It's astonishing to think that this indomitable bird, the fastest animal on the planet and the bird of noblemen, was very nearly wiped out in many areas around the world. The Peregrine Falcon has been persecuted by gamekeepers and egg collectors and has had chicks stolen to be sold on the black market for falconry. These incredible hunters were actively destroyed during World War II because they posed such a threat to the top-secret-note-carrying Messenger Pigeons they preyed upon and were practically extinct in the UK at one point. Add to that the herbicidal, chemical apocalypse of insecticide-containing DDT from the 1950s onwards, which thinned the bird's eggs, then our poor peregrines didn't stand a chance.

Thankfully due to conservation efforts these wonders of the world have been staging a steady fight for survival. So much so that they have moved from their rocky cliff sides to our town centres, nesting and breeding on cathedrals, hospitals and tower blocks. They are a wonderful sight for anyone who takes the time to look up. The fight isn't over for the Peregrine Falcon as it is still continually persecuted, so let's keep the dream alive and treasure this big, bold falcon as a symbol of resilience and hope for all our Red List birds.

WHAT CAN WE DO?

The reasons why 1 in 4 of our birds are endangered cannot be distilled down to any single factor. Their dwindling numbers are down to years of neglect and an aggressive push to squeeze more money out of the land rather than nurturing it. That being said, we can affect our own environments in positive ways that can immediately benefit the birds living alongside us. Bird boxes, feeders and baths are delightful ways to help them year-round as well as giving us the opportunity for good old bird spotting.

You can go even further by creating a wild flower garden to attract the bugs that birds are being forced to go without in the summer to help raise their young. It could be a patch of your garden dedicated to weeds and wild flowers, or just don't use the mower for a season and see if more birds stop by. You could also ask to have a small section of land at your school or place of work replanted and rewilded. Every little bit will help your local birds. From global matters like climate change and habitat loss, to help protecting the trees on your street and campaigning for native trees to be planted, you have a voice. If we all join in together, we will be heard.

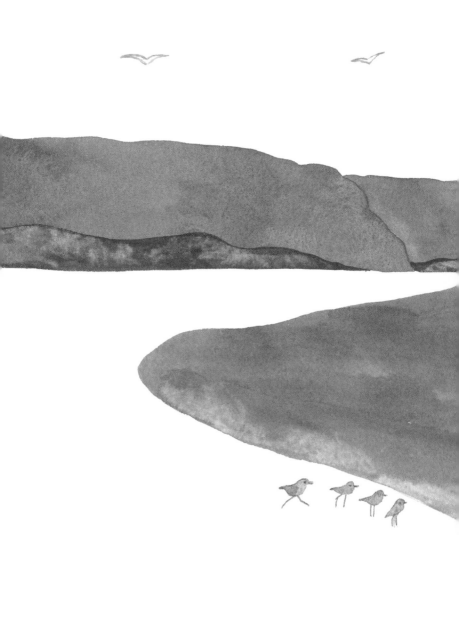

Chapter Three

COASTAL

Our coastlines are hugely dynamic ecosystems with diverse and unique inhabitants of animals, insects and marine plants all evolved to endure rapidly changing conditions and situations. Life seems like a beach to us when we are day-tripping for seaside holidays or surfing a left-hand offshore break; it's easy to think the natural world is in good health when you see the sky full of gulls and the rocky cliffs brimming with colonies of guillemots. But sadly, that isn't always the case.

Puffin

Fratercula arctica

The cover star of magazines, greetings cards, stamps, logos and calendars. Sea parrots that frolic, play and pounce on grassy hillocks like puppies, Puffins are also blisteringly good hunters of the cold, wild seas. Their only time spent on dry(ish) land is when they roost in burrows for breeding and they then head back out into the North Sea or Atlantic Ocean for the winter. For a funny little sea clown, that is hardcore!

A lot of the Puffin's traditional roosting islands off the coast of the western UK have grown quieter year after year and some are now totally devoid of the bird. It is believed that rising sea temperatures and overfishing of the Puffin's favoured sand eels and other delicacies have changed its habitat in a way that makes it unfeasible for it to live here. Fake plastic Puffins and piped Puffin calls from speakers have been placed in parts of the Isle of Man to try to encourage the birds back. With evidence that the birds are moving further north (there are more Puffins than people in Iceland, if you can believe it) and the fact that it is very hard to study them when they are alone far out to sea, it is thought that it is more a question of relocation than extinction. That doesn't mean we can ignore the Puffin's declining numbers though; if they continue to drop at the current rate, our amazing Puffin could quite easily go the way of the Dodo in the next 100 years.

Herring Gull

Larus argentatus

It might be a shock to find this mob on the Red List;
how can these seaside troublemaking, ploughed-field-
circling, landfill-scavenging, bin-bothering chip-stealers,
who seem to have pretty much evolved to make the
best of whatever situation they find themselves in,
be in decline? Their coastal population has halved in
the last 30 years but increased inland, which shows
how resilient these birds are; amazing aviators and
piscators, they are very canny birds who can read
humans well. They can stare right into your soul! So,
let's hope in years to come that the long, laugh-like call
of the Herring Gull is still as common on the coast as
the crashing waves of the eternal turn of the tides.

Kittiwake

Rissa tridactyla

Possibly our prettiest seabird, like the Cuckoo and Chiffchaff this gull calls out its own name. It is quite difficult to pick out in the clamour of a cliff of roosting birds, but if you visit the amazing inland colony in Newcastle upon Tyne where these lush seabirds nest on the quayside buildings, you will be able to hear how they sound so splendidly different from the rest of our coastal squawking. Putting appearances aside, these birds are hardy seafarers and as tough as a fisherman's boots but sadly their numbers have been decreasing over the last 20 years, as Kittiwakes mainly feed upon sand eels, like Puffins, seals and many other diving birds. Unfortunately, us pesky humans have also caught on to the oily sand eels and they are fished extensively for fish food, health supplements, animal feed and even used as fuel for power stations. So, overfishing, as well as changing sea temperatures displacing the eels, have had a dangerous knock-on effect that has already hit these gorgeous seabirds.

Long-tailed Duck

Clangula hyemalis

These small sea-ducks look like they are designed to sit prettily in ornamental ponds surrounded by lily pads and orchids, not out at sea braving breakers and riding the surf whipped by spindrift. The males have striking contrasting plumage during spring until their winter wetsuit comes back on, like a rolled-up protective hood, and the bird becomes almost entirely black. Visiting our northernmost eastern shores, little is known about this big wave rider, but studies show their numbers have dropped around the world. Oil spills from tankers can have a massive effect on this bird's feathers and even small amounts can render them useless in protecting against the cold. The oil can also clog the bird's stomach after preening. For any bird who spends as much time on the sea as the Long-tailed Duck, such spills, big or small, can be deadly.

Balearic Shearwater

Puffinus mauretanicus

Why would a Balearic bird that sounds like it would normally be sat in an Ibizan bar sipping cocktails as the sun sets get a mention here? This bird of passage breeds in the Mediterranean and then takes to the wing; shearwaters are famed for massive migrations and some, like the Manx Shearwater, cross oceans and continents. Travelling seaward around western Europe, the Balearic occasionally winters in UK waters. Although they are extremely rare, these birds are as much part of our rich tapestry of life as any other. The fact that they are the only globally critically endangered bird species in the UK (and that they're more endangered than tigers and pandas) should be regarded as much our concern as those in the Mediterranean and the rest of the world.

White-tailed Sea Eagle

Haliaeetus albicilla

It is with much delight that we can once again call
the White-tailed Sea Eagle a British bird. The fourth
largest eagle in the world, with huge wings like ferry
bow doors and a white tail that flashes like a yacht's
sail, this fantastical bird of prey was reintroduced in
Scotland in the 1980s and has been slowly going from
strength to strength. Historically, like many raptors,
this eagle was seen as a threat to livestock and hunting
and was all but wiped out. Some barely hung on but
like our Peregrine Falcon (see page 53), Red Kite (see
page 139) and Hen Harrier (see page 122), they have
fared better in the last decade after a string of recovery
programmes. With chicks from Scandinavia brought to
the UK and successfully raised on the beautiful west
coast and the Isle of Wight, they have made a powerful
comeback. Hopefully we will see more around the
rest of our coastline soon — they do like to travel.

Roseate Tern

Sterna dougallii

In the UK, the Roseate Tern breeds in only one location — the small Coquet Island in Northumberland. This makes this tern the rarest breeding seabird in the UK and one of the rarest in Europe. They have the classic tern look: sleek long wings and tail feathers with ice-white bodies offset wonderfully by a black cap, red feet and beak. In summer their chests are blushed pink, giving them the rose in their name. Any population of birds that is restricted to one location is at immense risk from predators and disease — just think of all the species in New Zealand lost to rats and domestic pets when westerners settled there. Luckily these terns are now a protected species, and everything is being done to make them stronger for the future — including invaluable work done by the Roseate Tern Life Project.

Shag

Phalacrocorax aristotelis

The coastal seafaring Shag should not be mistaken for the much more common Cormorant, being from the same family they look practically identical apart from the Shag's fantastic quiff and emerald-green eyes. It is the Cormorant that you may have spotted at inland watering destinations, holding aloft their dark wings to dry in the sun. This sinister look is practised by all cormorants because, unlike a lot of seabirds, their wings aren't waterproof. Rather than trapping air, water flows through feathers with ease, which is a helpful aid when it comes to diving for food. This is something they excel at: they are famed hunters who will eat anything, including discarded fishing equipment and the dreaded microplastics. Sadly, these divers also rely heavily on the sand eel family for a huge portion of their diet and, like many other seabirds, this has caused a decline in their population as sand eels have decreased in number.

WHAT CAN WE DO?

With water covering 70 per cent of the planet, protecting our seas is a global issue. We need governments to work together to protect, conserve and fight against climate change as a collective. We need to keep protective environmental rules and regulations in place to conserve our own coastlines and to be able to fight against overfishing so we can live happily alongside seabirds and all sea life. We also need to be able to work together for cleaner water, just like Surfers Against Sewage did in the 1990s to great effect.

Individually, organised beach cleans are vitally important for our coastal birds. It may not seem like much, but just picking up that plastic water bottle cap will prevent it being ground up into microplastics and dispersed back into the sea to be ingested by organisms that are then eaten by fish, who are then eaten by a bigger fish and then caught by a bird. So, by doing a little litter picking you are helping out in a big way. The Surfers Against Sewage website and social media channels are great places to help find a beach clean near you that you can participate in.

Chapter Four

FARMLAND

With rolling fields, neat hedgerows and smooth hills like snooker tables, it's easy to see our Great British countryside as a bucolic wonderland — surely it must be teeming with life? Sadly not. Over the past 40 years agriculture has intensified, and working side by side with nature has vanished. In its place has risen a style of mass production that does not care for wildness or the animals that survive in the fields and the spaces between. Gone are life-rich hedgerows and non-profit-making wild spaces. The loss in abundance is stark. Pesticides have killed off so many bugs that it is apocalyptic; a couple of decades ago a drive in the countryside would have splattered your windscreen with all kinds of creepy crawlies, but now the bonnet will be as clean as a kingfisher's beak. We are seeing the results of years of these farming practices in bird surveys and their brutal readings; every countryside bird with a few exemptions (Jackdaws, Rooks, Goldfinches and Wood Pigeons) have been hit hard and place on the Red List. We can't just blame mass agriculture though; market forces are also responsible for this high-octane growth.

Turtle Dove
Streptopelia turtur

The migratory Turtle Dove holds the unwanted title of our fastest declining Red List bird, with a 93 per cent drop since 1970. These birds endure an epic journey that begins in sub-Saharan Africa, travelling over land and sea, battling illegal netters and hunters in the Mediterranean, and other avian dangers to take roost in the farmland of southern England. Utterly exhausted from this migration, the birds often struggle to find the right habitat to roost, which ultimately leads to a decline in their numbers. The Turtle Dove needs tall trees to nest, wild flower seed to feed and some kind of pond or water to drink from; it's not much to ask but these are increasingly hard to find. Thankfully, Operation Turtle Dove has sprung up to aid our doves and create initiatives for farmers to free up some space for nature with much-needed 'wild' corners of their land. Success stories such as the Knepp Castle Estate continue to home the Turtle Dove. Bravo!

Skylark

Alauda arvensis

The Skylark is as much of a symbol of rural Britain as the Robin is of a jolly Christmas, but not many would recognise this buff-streaked, spiky-haired, stocky songbird. This bird really is all about the song, heard by ramblers, lovers holding hands, farmers chewing hay, and in the minds of the World War I soldiers in the trenches dreaming of home. It is a song of freedom. Skylarks exist in that grey area between the moors and farmland, where the grass is long and they can fly up propelled by their song and sing and sing. Unfortunately more and more of this land is being cultivated, destroying the lark's perfect habitat. With the main ploughing season coinciding with their second and third broods, which Skylarks need to keep their population stable, their nests are simply crushed, or exposed and left open to predation. Thankfully all this harm can be reversed, but only if landowners make the effort to do so.

Cirl Bunting

Emberiza cirlus

It may be on the Red List but the burly Cirl Bunting is a farmland success story. Once widespread across the rural south of England, the birds gradually started to disappear as intensive farming increased until they were practically extinct in the UK by the 1970s, only breeding in tiny areas of Devon and Cornwall. These sedentary birds could not adapt and shrunk with their habitat until the RSPB bought land in their ranges and reintroduced the wild flowers and winter crops needed to sustain them. These small patches of land not only helped bring the Cirls back from the brink of extinction, but increased their numbers by 800 per cent as well as creating stunning meadows to boot. Further life has also sprung up in these places as rare flowers, mammals and other birds reap the rewards of this valuable ecosystem — and it was so simple to do. Surely many lessons can be learned from the success of our humble Cirls.

Corncrake

Crex crex

People of my parent's generation talk about the Corncrakes of their youth like I have spoken of the Lapwings of mine (see page 93). These incredibly rare birds have been pushed further and further north on their migratory flight from Africa by intensive, land-draining farming methods and can now only find home on secluded Scottish isles. It seems unimaginable that they could once have been heard loud and clear all across Great Britain. These secretive birds — no bigger than the Moorhen they are related to — are known for their 'crex'-ing call, sung relentlessly through the summer nights like cicadas. It is devastating to think that these rails are quickly becoming a creature of the past, but happily conservation groups have been set up to protect the Corncrake and the habitat on its favoured islands, so all hope is not lost.

Linnet

Linaria cannabina

Our unassuming Linnet is one of my unsung heroes;
I always seem to spot one when I really need to — they are
my little spirit-raising animal. The male's pink, grey and
beige plumage gives the impression that they have made
an effort to look smart, but it's not really in them. Best to
just take them as they come. To spot them browsing among
wild flowers and hedgerows on a summer day is a delight;
it's this plant life that these finches love most of all, feeding
almost exclusively on the seeds of weeds that poke through
in spaces between crops. But these plants are becoming
increasingly harder to find on farmland due to fields being
conglomerated through the removal of hedgerows and the
widespread use of weedkillers.

Lapwing

Vanellus vanellus

I don't want to sound like some boring old bloke (I'm not that old for a start) but when I was a kid I remember seeing fields full of Lapwings. You may still be able to see big flocks in flight gathered for winter, but those peewits of old have gone. These beautiful waders who are just as at home on estuaries, scrapes and marshes as they are on farmland have a lot going for them: iridescent plumage perfect for camouflage and pied wings that give an undulating effect while flying. They also have a nifty trick up their sleeve: a pretend broken wing tactic to lure danger away from their young and that famous and distinct 'peewit' call. But still, even with all of these special powers, the Lapwing is disappearing. Large-scale farming has not just stretched into their traditional breeding habitat but also drained it and pumped it with herbicides and pesticides, plus the late-summer ploughing of fields can destroy a whole brood in seconds.

Thankfully, there is a massive UK-wide scheme to restore our natural environment via a fully integrated natural network, using massive corridors of wilderness across the country to link key areas and provide the perfect conditions for our wildlife to flourish once again. Fingers crossed it comes sooner rather than later.

Yellowhammer

Emberiza citrinella

The colour of a summer sun and buttercup chins, with a song that dances out of hedgerows, down paths and into the fields, like their own startled flight. These birds are full of rustic charm and are found across the country in the in-between grasslands that merge with farmland and in the hedgerows that outline our countryside like a permanent marker. These are all places that are slowly getting gobbled up by industrial farming unless protected, so understandably this habitat loss has led to a decline in Yellowhammers. Thankfully, the RSPB have proved that making some simple changes to farming practices can help to save Yellowhammers (and many other farm birds). Providing nest opportunities by cutting hedgerows less, ensuring there is both summer food (having wild flower areas to feed both adults and chicks) and winter food (growing small batches of over-winter crops) are key steps. Just these three things have instantly helped the Yellowhammer begin to thrive again, so imagine if all farms took on such responsibilities. It is a lot to ask but some companies, like the cereal maker Jordan's, only work with farms that provide such wild habitats as a matter of course. This surely must be the future.

Tree Sparrow

Passer montanus

They could easily be mistaken for one another, but the Tree Sparrow doesn't look half as grumpy as its cousin the House Sparrow. It is wonderfully attired with a chestnut conker cap, organic cottagecore colours and a distinctive black spot on the cheek that sometimes looks like thick farmhand-like sideburns. The main difference is that you won't really see the Tree Sparrow around your house or town in the UK — they are very much country mice, preferring to loiter round farmland, hedgerows and scattered trees.

It is quite likely you have never seen a Tree Sparrow, even as common as they once were; they have sadly suffered a huge loss in numbers, over 90 per cent in the last 30 years. Their dwindling presence is likely due to the loss of their breeding habitat and agricultural changes and the removal and constant 'tidying' of the hedgerows that divide fields and line our roads. Although these hedgerows are the ideal environment for a quarrel of sparrows to raise their young, luckily the Tree Sparrow also takes well to nesting boxes and there are vital organisations in key areas that have been set up to help rehome these lovely little birds. Hopefully projects like these, and a scruffier attitude to our hedgerows and verges, will help their numbers rise again.

WHAT CAN WE DO?

Not all farms use excessive practices on their land, starving the soil of minerals and destroying habitats, but do. Farmers are the custodians of some of our most treasured and threatened birds' environments. Luckily, there is a lot that they can do; not cutting hedges in spring and leaving wild spaces for native flowers to thrive and attract insects for food for raising their chicks makes a huge difference to our birds. Leaving sections of land uncultivated for ground-nesting birds and not draining land also provides valuable drinking water.

In a new initiative called Land Sparing farms remove the borders to create one large field to farm intensively. They use the land freed up to create another wild field for birds. Winter is the hardest time for birds but farmers can help by planting winter crops for them and leaving stubble from the previous crop, encouraging insects and foraging. The real key is cutting down on the use of pesticides; even though many chemicals have been banned, toxicity is still high, so natural defences must be considered. Birds eat insects, so what could possibly be better pest control than a field full of finches?

Chapter Five

WETLAND

Mainly hidden away in long, flat expanses of land, we don't really see most of our wetlands and estuaries as they are quite often inaccessible to us landlubbers. Wetlands make up only 3 per cent of our land but home around 10 per cent of our wildlife: otters, fish, frogs, toads, newts, bats, water voles, snakes, dragonflies, water spiders, lots of flies, and plenty of birds to eat the bugs. Herons, swans, harriers, kingfishers and warblers galore are found in these alien landscapes alongside legions of geese and waders that have flown for thousands of miles to call our land home for a season or two. Luckily there are protected areas of wetland dotted with hides around the country so we can experience the wildlife that would normally come and go so surreptitiously — apart from the massive honking flying Vs of geese practising for their migration south in the winter. Unfortunately, an increasing amount of our wild wetland is degrading due to poor management and pollution, causing harm to the whole ecosystem that relies on these wonderful bogs.

Cuckoo

Cuculus canorus

Perhaps the most famous of all bird song; everybody knows it, but the Cuckoo is getting rarer and rarer by the year. It arrives here early in the year, heralding in spring after a perilous journey, and faces great challenges of survival once it arrives too. The use of pesticides is believed to have greatly reduced food sources for the Cuckoo, whether adult or newly hatched and plumped up by its adopted parents who are tasked with raising the chick after the mother secretly lays an egg in their nest. Climate change is also believed to be a factor in their decline; certain Cuckoo hosts such as Meadow Pipits, Dunnocks and Reed Warblers are nesting ever so slightly later in the year. This off-kilter timing is no doubt effecting the Cuckoo's egg laying. It is also likely that there is another climate-related interference on the bird's epic journey from Africa to Europe and Asia that is harming them along the way, but this is much harder to study.

Ruff

Calidris pugnax

These wonderful waders are mainly summer migrants
found around our coastline, although East Anglia has
habitually homed a small population of breeding Ruffs.
Outside of springtime, our male here would look like
any other sandpiper, browsing the shoreline or lakeside
pebbly patches for molluscs and titbits. Come the breeding
season however, he has a dramatic costume change and
dons a fanciful plumage of red, black, white, ochre and
blue feathers. These look almost exactly like the ruffs
and powdered wigs of a sixteenth-century nobleman,
and are proudly displayed. The leks that males gather
in to parade and fight for breeding rights can look
like a boozy brawl at a fancy-dress party. The Ruff is
one of a handful of species of birds that partake in
this ritual that was once a widespread occurrence but
due to the draining of fenland over the last 300 years
we have been left with literally a handful of breeding
couples. Everything must be done to protect the land
and to keep the Ruff's customs, hopefully encouraging
even more to join in their eye-catching displays.

Bittern

Botaurus stellaris

These strange herons of the underworld are famously rare; in the nineteenth century they were hunted and considered a delicacy, then brought back from near extinction by repopulating the UK with European bitterns only then to be once again nearly wiped out by shooting, egg collectors and finally the drainage of their home marshlands. Their distinguishing booming call became a symbol of scarcity and by the 1990s the Bittern was considered an ancient wonder of the natural world that would be lost in time. But due to years of conservation work, and in a glorious upturn, the Bittern has been successfully removed from the Red List and placed on the Amber List. Bitterns are amazing birds and their story shows the importance of conservation areas and why the protective rules that have been made in Europe must be kept in place, enforced and funded, however our nation changes over the coming years. Long live the Bittern!

Grey Wagtail

Motacilla cinerea

The wild swimmer's friend. They bounce, weave and bob just like the fast-flowing bubbly water they are found next to, hopping from bankside, to boulder, to branch, catching bugs that thrive on the water's edge. But why call this bird grey when they have a beautiful patch of powdered-acid yellow and so many other lovely characteristics?

I have found the Grey Wagtail to be a relatively common spot over the years and one that has never failed to pluck my heart strings, so it was shocking to see that it has been placed on the Red List, despite our waterways being much cleaner now than they were 30 years ago. It is largely unknown why there has been such a drop in the breeding population but, as always, the key factors of climate change and habitat loss must be taken into consideration.

Yellow Wagtail

Motacilla flava

The Yellow Wagtail is just so utterly yellow that it really couldn't have been called anything else. Sorry Grey; please don't take it personally.

These migrant birds travel from Africa to nest and breed in our boggy agricultural lands, arriving to align their chick rearing with peak greenness and to catch the bugs that come with high summer. Sadly, the Yellow Wagtail has suffered one of the largest declines of our summer breeding birds with a nearly 50 per cent decrease in numbers over the past 20 years. This is because their preferred habitat of wet farmland has greatly diminished over the same period. Drained to be converted to arable pasture or to yield more of produce, the fields and watering holes that were once plentiful have all but disappeared. This loss has taken with it the insects that Yellow Wagtails desperately need to raise their chicks and the habitat that can protect their young rather than leaving them exposed to predation. They simply cannot survive in their old homes any more with not enough to eat or drink.

Aquatic Warbler

Acrocephalus paludicola

If it wasn't for the excited clamour of twitchers, this highly secretive bird would come and go from Britain completely unnoticed. These rare autumn-passage birds make their way back to West Africa with stop-offs in southern UK fenland. With its tiger-striped plumage, the Aquatic Warbler can remain hidden in the long reeds totally obscured from sight, but it is these stripes that make the bird such a rare and cherished spot as these markings distinguish it from its lookalike, the much more common Sedge Warbler.

Sadly, the Aquatic Warbler is globally threatened: habitat loss throughout Europe has caused a drastic fall in the bird's numbers, with so much fenland being drained for agriculture it is becoming critical that land is preserved to keep our global treasures safe. However, sadly, like the Golden Oriole (see page 28), Red-backed Shrike (see page 134) and Wryneck, this may be one species we have already lost. Hopefully, as we re-wild our wetlands, we might see the return of Aquatic Warbler.

Savi's Warbler
& Grasshopper Warbler

Locustella luscinioides & Locustella naevia

Warblers are hard enough to tell apart at the best of times, so using your ears is your best chance of making the distinction, especially when the birds are hidden in a cryptic maze of reeds and rushes, where getting even just a little glimpse is virtually impossible. These two marshland dwellers sound amazingly alike too, both with long strange, clicking calls, but it's with the Grasshopper Warbler's persistent and insect-like song that you will be able to spot the difference. The Savi is the much scarcer of these two birds as the UK is just on the outer limits of its breeding zone, so a nesting pair is an extremely rare and amazing spot. The Grasshopper Warbler has always been a much greater feature of the UK's ecosystem and, like many other migrant summer birds with specific habitat requirements both here and in its wintering grounds, it has taken a big hit in population over the last 30 years.

WHAT CAN WE DO?

This definitely has to be my favourite suggestion for what we can do to help protect our Red List birds — introducing beavers to help establish and maintain wetlands, create rich and diverse ecosystems, improve water quality and even prevent flooding. What's not to like?

Across Europe, beavers have been released back into the wild with the help of special conservation projects, of which we need more! Beavers felling trees creates more light in those areas, helping smaller trees grow and bringing a wealth of nesting and feeding opportunities for birds. Beavers use gnawed branches to create dams to make big pools of water, which they use as escape routes from predators and to feed on aquatic plants. In turn, these lagoons attract fish, amphibians and insects — *lots of insects* — that then attract more birds. It's vital to create new, food-rich habitats not just for our birds but for all kinds of mammals too. It's amazing to think that all this can be done by just a few beavers. Friends of the Earth have been working hard to get more introduced in the UK; you can support them and campaign locally with Wildlife Trusts to bring some closer to your home.

Chapter Six

UPLAND

Those high, wild places: home to only savage beasts, drifters and couples in cagoules with OS maps and flasks. It is true that the UK does have some very dangerous habitats for the unprepared, but most of our uplands are as managed and manicured as everywhere else in the country. With 40 per cent of the land described as upland, there is a lot to go round; these massive tracts are home to tourism and recreation, deer and grouse shoots, and forestry and farming. They are also places of imagination, wonder and inspiration. Over the decades, they have helped artists and writers to create masterpieces and they offer relaxation and fresh air to the townsfolk who constantly make their way there every weekend or school holiday to relish their own version of freedom.

Hen Harrier

Circus cyaneus

We are up in arms when we see social media posts about traditional bird hunting and illegal netting that takes place all around Europe; we are disgusted when we watch blue-chip nature programmes highlighting the hunting of animals to near extinction in far-off places, it's an outrage! But what most people don't know is that the same thing is happening right here under our noses to an incredible bird of prey called the Hen Harrier and our government is turning a blind eye. All harriers cut an amazing silhouette in the sky, but the rare Hen Harrier has always inspired awe with its pastel grey and black ink-dipped plumage, the way it patrols moorland with ease and dances in the spring skies. As the name suggests, it favours ground birds; Red Grouse being particularly high on the menu, which doesn't go down well on the vast swathes of land managed for grouse shoots. Never mind snatching prey, just the mere presence of the Hen Harrier can spook the Grouse to hide and completely ruin the day's shoot. So, persecution is high; over the previous two years, 44 Hen Harriers have been killed or gone missing under suspicious circumstances on land designated for driven grouse shoots. That number is likely to be higher by the time you're reading this. These birds are highly protected and tagged, so satellite tracking shows exactly where they are killed and suggests who the culprits are. The future of the Hen Harrier almost certainly depends on the licensing of private grouse moors, and that is a future we must continue to fight for.

Black Grouse

Lyrurus tetrix

Hello handsome! These highland heart-throbs of the heather were at one time found in the uplands too, from John O'Groats to Land's End, but now like many of our wildest birds they have been pushed further and further north as their habitats have diminished. The females are a tweed-like mottled grey and the males a midnight blue-black with red eyebrow wattles and an incredible Lyrebird-like fan tail. These appendages are propelled and presented with incredibly boastful displays among the males when they meet in leks, fighting and parading to win the affection of the females — the toughest gets the chicks. The moorland is the arena and the grouse are our superstars; it is an incredible shame that such sporting events are so rare they can only really now be viewed on the TV or online as due to the loss of basics such as food and housing, the Black Grouse's numbers are so low they are now on the Red List. Thankfully habitat management is underway in certain areas and the grouse are strengthening, so hopefully the Black Grouse versus Black Grouse showdown is a spectacle soon to be viewed by the many and not just the few.

Grey Partridge

Perdix perdix

You could have a look in a pear tree to see if there's a Grey Partridge there, but you will probably find that that rotund bird is actually a fat Wood Pigeon. In fact, if you're looking for the Grey Partridge, don't look up in the trees at all as they prefer the ground where farmland meets the hills. A hundred years ago, this game bird was incredibly abundant; there were millions of them on estates and low moorland across the country. A perfect hunting bird with their low flight and loud call; thousands could be killed in a shoot in just a couple of days. So, come the present day, their numbers do not even reach 40,000. It would be easy to think that they have simply all been shot, but the use of herbicides has also eradicated the insects that their chicks are raised on, which means that, like many of our other countryside birds, the chicks don't survive to adulthood.

Procedures, such as chick-rearing habitats and winter feeding grounds, are in place to try to reverse the decline; fingers crossed it's not too late.

Capercaillie

Tetrao urogallus

These utterly magnificent Scottish game birds are big and bold as brass and have always been considered so with their ancient Gaelic name, which means 'Horse of the Woods'. They are intimidating in flight, in voice and on foot, especially during mating season when they are highly territorial and will battle other males to win breeding rights in the area. Our largest grouse has already paid the price of over-hunting and habitat loss in the past. In the eighteenth century, the Capercaillie was wiped out by shoots and the deforestation of their pine homelands in the Scottish highlands. They thrived once again in the following century after a project reintroducing birds from Sweden was successful, but sadly as we begin this century these amazing birds are on the brink of extinction again. Although highly protected, the Capercaillie's numbers continue to drop due to the historic loss of breeding ranges and the over-grazing of their forest food by sheep and deer. Sheep are handy for keeping grass short, but this over-grazing halts the regeneration of new growth. So much has been done to help protect the bird over the years and now a massive undertaking is underway to connect ancient breeding grounds across Scotland with green bridges of pine trees. By connecting mature forests in this way, we will give the Capercaillie and many other mammals and birds a wide range of land and protection, and a greater hope of survival.

Dotterel

Charadrius morinellus

These beautiful cinnamon and burnt umber waders are a bit of an anomaly in the bird world for a variety of reasons. They are quite often spotted on passage from North Africa to Scandinavia at regular coastal hotspots, but the birds that choose to stay and breed here do so in the highlands of Scotland and England, nesting in the high plateaux of mountains. Not only that, the boldest and brightest plumage belongs to the female pictured here, who after laying and sitting on the eggs for a short while, leaves the rest of the brooding and chick rearing to the male. She is then free to head off and maybe have another clutch or two with another Dotterel. As modern as this sounds, it is an amazing survival tactic if you are designed to thrive in the mountainous regions of the world and with international numbers of the bird falling, such bright ideas are critical.

Merlin

Falco columbarius

A Kestrel for a knave, a Merlin for a lady. You can see why: Merlins are small, cute and perfectly formed hunters of grey-blue and blushed pink. The two birds are very alike but the Merlin doesn't have the hovering prowess of the Kestrel as they prefer to hunt on the wing, dropping to catch birds at ground level. Sadly the Merlin is a much rarer bird, as recently as 50 years ago it was nearly wiped out due to the widespread use of pesticides, which created a cocktail of adverse effects for many birds. These included physical harm, weight loss, reduced fertility and hatchability of eggs as well as the loss of insect bio-abundance that works its way to the peak of the food chain. Thankfully, due to a reduction in certain chemical formulas and the use of herbicides in the 1980s, the Merlin's numbers have been rising year on year. It is still on the Red List but the future is looking bright.

Red-backed Shrike

Lanius collurio

I can hold my hands up and say that as a child I was terrified of shrikes; the butcher bird that eats any animal of any size and brutally stores their kills in grim hawthorn-spiked cupboards, like a feathered Vlad the Impaler. My favourite illustrations are of them surrounded by lifeless frogs, stag beetles, mice, lizards and even other birds of the moors; not bad for a bird that is just a tad bigger than a Great Tit. The shrike's much hyped, big-game trophy hunting of mammals and reptiles is a bit of a misnomer, though. It is true that they catch them, but the birds need insects to survive. Bugs are their bread and butter, especially for their young and the loss of insects due to pesticides and other farming practices means that it is simply not sustainable for the Red-backed Shrike to breed here. Why migrate here all the way from Africa when there is simply nothing to eat? That is why the Red-backed Shrike, like the Golden Oriole (see page 28) and the Wryneck, is all but extinct in the UK apart from some seasonal migratory birds. So, I wish I could have told myself that there is nothing to be scared of about the shrike other than that they could easily be extinct within our lifetime.

Ring Ouzel

Turdus torquatus

This close relation of our homely Blackbird migrates here
from North Africa to breed every summer, feeding on
insects and juniper berries as it goes. Looking pretty much
identical to the Blackbird, apart from the white bib that
makes it look like a Blackbird wearing a napkin in
a fancy restaurant, the Ring Ouzel much prefers the
heather of the heathlands to the rowans of the town parks,
so their paths don't cross too much. It is not exactly known
why the Ouzel has had a 40 per cent drop in breeding
numbers over the last 40 years but it is safe to assume that
the decline in its British habitat must be having
a devastating effect on our visitor and so more must be
done to keep our frequent flyer returning year after year.

Twite

Linaria flavirostris

There has always been a place in my heart for our unassuming Pennine finch. I've usually considered myself quite shallow when it comes to birds, loving the bright and bold of our everyday avian friends, but the Twite has a quiet charm as it goes about its social duties while foraging on the heath of the uplands during the summer in its camouflaged wine-stained tweeds. Twites are always together before and after they set sail south for the coast to face out winter on muddy salt flats. Unfortunately, they are another of our small passerines whose numbers have plummeted over the last 40 years. Upland management and restoration projects have been put in place to keep key areas of the finch's habitat in appropriate condition, but sadly this has not turned events. However, thanks to the bright minds of Twite conservationists, attention has been turned to the bird's favoured wintering grounds and extra special care has been taken to keep the Twite's coastal plants abundant to see them through the cold days and nights. We have to give our thanks to all the people who devote so much of their time to fight for the survival of our native birds, not just the grandstanders or big-name birds, but the ones you have never heard of, like our lovely Twite.

Red Kite

Milvus milvus

In medieval times Black Kites were widespread in towns
and cities; their love of carrion meant they were
a valuable asset in helping to keep the streets free of dead
animals. Back then, Red Kites were just as abundant
in the countryside. Sadly, persecution followed and
the birds were all but wiped out apart from a handful
of protected breeding pairs in Wales. Then back in the
1990s, a reintroduction programme was set up which has
flourished into one of the biggest conservation success
stories of the past 30 years. Now many skies in counties
around the country are dotted with the elegant and
enigmatic silhouette of this amazing bird of prey. And it is
always very special to spot a Red Kite in Wales knowing
its ancestor was one of the very few left on this land. It
should give us hope for all our species of birds.

WHAT CAN WE DO?

Driven grouse shooting is a blood sport unchecked like no other; it is an industry that openly survives on nature crimes. Every year Hen Harriers, Peregrines, Buzzards, Red Kites, Kestrels and more are slaughtered to protect young grouse and to keep the skies clear for shoots. It is part of an anti-conservationist approach to land management; burning peat to promote new growth of heather for the game birds releases tons of stored carbon into the atmosphere. It is keeping land barren that should be tree-filled and capable of soaking up the rain that now falls and floods the valleys below. This is not a gentleman's sport of stealth and cunning, and without regulation shoots do what they want to maximise the number of birds released and shot, to make the most money, without any regard for the wildlife that happens to live on these moors. If licensing can help to deter such flaunters of the law then the government must enforce this with large fines and prison time; if not, an outright ban on driven grouse shoots is the only thing that can help prevent this ongoing butchery of birds. Search online for petitions to have your voice heard and to help fight against these damning practises.

SPOTTING AND JOTTING

It's always exciting to see a bird you've never seen before. You can use these pages below to mark when you've spied one of the brilliant feathered friends mentioned in this book.

☐ Nightingale

☐ Marsh & Willow Tit

☐ Woodcock

☐ Hawfinch

☐ Pied Flycatcher &
Spotted Flycatcher

☐ Golden Oriole

☐ Lesser Spotted
Woodpecker

☐ Lesser Redpoll

☐ Fieldfare & Redwing

☐ Wood Warbler

☐ Nightjar

☐ Song Thrush

☐ Cuckoo

☐ Starling

☐ Mistle Thrush

☐ Puffin

☐ Black Redstart

☐ House Sparrow

☐ Balearic Shearwater

☐ Peregrine Falcon

☐ Linnet

☐ Skylark

☐ White-tailed Sea Eagle

☐ Shag

☐ Roseate Tern

□ Cirl Bunting

□ Long-tailed Duck

□ Turtle Dove

☐ Corncrake

☐ Lapwing

☐ Kittiwake

☐ Tree Sparrow

☐ Yellowhammer

☐ Herring Gull

☐ Ruff

☐ Aquatic Warbler

☐ Bittern

☐ Black Grouse

☐ Grey Partridge

☐ Hen Harrier

☐ Grey Wagtail

☐ Yellow Wagtail

☐ Capercaillie

☐ Merlin

☐ Savi's Warbler
  & Grasshopper Warbler

☐ Dotterel

☐ Red Kite

☐ Ring Ouzel

☐ Red-backed Shrike

☐ Twite

THANKS

To the Sewells, Roses, Lees & the Avery-O'Sullivans

Melissa Harrison, Jamie Dunning, Dan Wrench,
Nancy 'The Natural Gardener' Lowe,
Chris Packham, Mark Avery, Yolo Birder,
Chris Sharpe and Kelvin Cooper

Cirl Bunting Reintroduction Conservation Project
Surfers Against Sewage
Tyne Kittiwake Partnership
Operation Turtle Dove
Curlew Country
Rewilding Britain
Friends of the Earth
Back From The Brink